ESCAPE FROM ALCATRAZ

THE MYSTERY OF THE THREE MEN
WHO ESCAPED FROM THE ROCK

BY ERIC BRAUN

CAPSTONE PRESS
a capstone imprint

Encounter is published by Capstone Press, a Capstone imprint,
1710 Roe Crest Drive, North Mankato, Minnesota 56003
www.mycapstone.com

Library of Congress Cataloging-in-Publication Data is available on the
Library of Congress website
ISBN 978-1-5157-4551-8 (reinforced library hardcover)
ISBN 978-1-5157-4552-5 (paperback)
ISBN 978-1-5157-4553-2 (eBook PDF)

Editorial Credits

Mandy Robbins, editor; Russell Griesmer, designer; Wanda Winch, media
researcher; Tori Abraham, production specialist

Photo Credits

Christin Gordova, 100 (bottom); Courtesy Golden Gate National
Recreation Area: GOGA 17934.038, 101 (top), GOGA 404, 107 (t), GOGA
405, 106 (b), GOGA 406, 106 (t), GOGA 407, 106 (middle), GOGA 408
and 409, 104 (b), Betty Wallar Photograph Collection 1935-1960, GOGA
19200.340, 101 (b), Don DeNevi Photograph Collection, GOGA-17975.21,
103 (t); Federal Bureau of Investigations, cover (mug shots), 71, 103
(b), 104 (t), 105 (t), chapter opener design using elements from wanted
posters used on pages 4, 14, 24, 32, 44, 52, 62, 72, 82, 92; Getty
Images: Bettmann, 99 (b); Ocean View Publishing, 23, 43, 98 (b), 99
(t), 102 (all), 105 (b); Reuters: U.S. Department of Justice/Handout,
107 (b); Shutterstock: donatas1205, stucco wall background, Fosin,
cover (light burst), freeart, parchment paper design, ilolab, old
gray paper design, kropic1, 98 (t), marchello74, white-brick design,
mexrix, tape pieces design, Mikhail Grachikov, cover (glowing line
design), Naaman Abreu, 95, Nejron Photo, cover (clouds), 1 (clouds),
Paladin12, old paper design, Paisan Changhirun, cover (rain), 1 (rain),
StrelaStudio, brick wall design, T.W., cover (Alcatraz Island),
TaraPatta, crumbling wall design, Vladislav Gajic, cover (ocean
surface), 1 (ocean surface); Wikimedia: Uzma Gamal, 100 (t)

Printed in Canada.
010034S17

TABLE OF CONTENTS

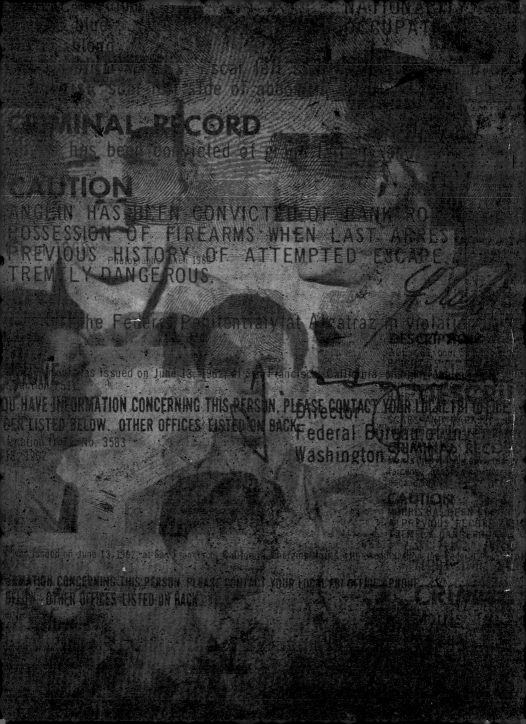

CHAPTER 1

SOUND THE ALARM!

At the crack of dawn, Cellblock B in the Alcatraz Federal Penitentiary was silent and dark. Clarence Carnes, a longtime prisoner, lay on his bunk, already awake. He'd barely slept all night. Suddenly, the wake-up bell rang out, just as it did every morning, and the prisoners began to stir. They had 15 minutes to get out of bed, go to the bathroom, and get dressed. Some stayed in bed to grab a few extra minutes of sleep.

After 15 minutes a whistle pierced the air, and the prisoners walked to the front of their cells. It was time for the morning head count.

Carnes was one of the first inmates at the front of his cell. He stood eagerly at the bars and looked around.

He listened as the guards walked down the aisle and counted prisoners one at a time. He had reason to believe that the count might be short this morning. His friends had planned a daring overnight escape from the "escape-proof" prison. He hoped they had made it.

What Carnes heard next made his heart leap. One of the guards called for a recount. It was possible that the guard had simply made a mistake and needed to count again. But Carnes didn't think so. His friends were smart, and they had a good plan. They had been working on their escape for months and had been painstaking about every last detail. Right now, Carnes imagined, they were breathing fresh outside air. He suppressed a smile as Officer Lawrence Bartlett, the guard on duty, counted again.

Officer Bartlett soon noticed that prisoner John, "J.W.," Anglin had not gotten up. He walked over, reached between the bars, and tapped the prisoner's pillow. But Anglin did not respond. Bartlett called Lieutenant Bill Long down for a look. He told Long that Anglin was either dead — or he had been replaced by a life-sized dummy.

Long poked Anglin's head. Still, Anglin just lay there. He poked it again, harder, and this time his fingers pushed right through. Startled, he swatted the head, and it rolled off the bunk onto the floor. It *was* a dummy! Long jumped back.

Long reached through the bars, yanked the blanket down, and saw rolled up blankets and clothes that Anglin had placed there to look like his body. He quickly went to the next cell, that of Clarence Anglin, John's brother, and pulled off his blanket. Clarence's bed was also filled with blankets and a fake head. There was one more prisoner missing from the head count — Frank Morris. Long dashed over to Morris's cell and pulled the covers off his dummy head and blankets. He was gone too!

A call was made to acting Warden Arthur Dollison. He lived in a duplex on the island with his family. When the phone rang in his home, Dollison felt a chill of dread go through him. It could not be good news to get a phone call right after the morning count. As he and more officers rushed to the cellblock, an escape alarm blared throughout the prison and all across the island, indoors and out.

Adding to the commotion, another prisoner was calling out to the guards from his cell.

"I planned the entire escape," Allen West cried out. In his hands he held what looked like a vent cover, only it was made of cardboard.

Meanwhile, officers climbed up on top of Cellblock B, which was constructed of prison cells stacked three-high. Looking up, they saw a roof vent that had its bars removed. The prisoners had gone through there. The vent shaft led to the roof and was capped by a rain hood. But when officers got to the roof, they saw that the rain hood had been knocked aside. On the north side of the building, barbed wire had been cut from the fence. Outside the fence, the grass was matted down as if people had been there. The officers could hardly believe their eyes. "The Rock," the impenetrable fortress of Alcatraz, had been breached.

Dozens of officers fanned out all over the island. They searched the cell house, the workshops, storerooms, and other buildings. They checked an old dungeon below the cell house. They scoured the beaches, tramped through shrubbery, and inspected the caves along the shore. By boat, they patrolled the water around the island looking for bodies in the cold, churning sea.

At this point, Alcatraz officers realized that Frank Morris, John Anglin, and Clarence Anglin were most likely not on the island anymore. They called the San Francisco office of the FBI and informed them of what had happened. The FBI alerted the local police, the California Highway Patrol, the U.S. Navy, the U.S. Coast Guard, and all the sheriffs' offices in the area. A search was begun by land, air, and sea. It was 7:55 a.m., about 40 minutes after the morning head count, and a federal investigation was underway.

Back in Cellblock B, officers questioned other prisoners, including Clarence Carnes and Allen West. Years later, Carnes claimed to know a lot about the escape. He said he had helped Morris and the Anglin brothers with several details. But he kept his mouth shut at the time and hoped others would too. Many prisoners had learned about the escape. They had heard the men digging in their cells at night. But nobody said a word to the officers.

The situation was different for West. In the back of his cell, where there should have been an air vent, was a gaping hole. He had chipped away the concrete around the vent and knocked it out, and he had created a fake vent cover from cardboard. It was obvious that West was supposed to escape with the others, but something had gone wrong for him. He knew he could not hide his involvement with the plan, so he gave short answers to the officers' questions. But he was careful not to reveal too much. Chances are he didn't want to sabotage his friends' shot at freedom.

While West was being questioned in the warden's office, the rest of the cell house was searched. Up above Cellblock B, investigators noticed that blankets had been hung from the bars that enclosed the area between the top of the cellblock and the ceiling. What they found behind the blankets was stunning — a secret workshop full of tools, including a homemade wrench, a foot-long file, a stapler, a mirror, a flashlight, three spoon handles, and more. They also found a rubber raft and a life preserver, both of which the prisoners had made out of raincoats and left behind for West. There was even a vacuum cleaner motor that the prisoners had used to power a drill.

In Frank Morris's cell, they found magazine articles that explained how to make rafts and life jackets. John Anglin's cell contained art supplies and the paint that had been used on the dummy heads. Clarence Anglin's cell had knots of human hair left over from the dummy heads, and more paint.

One of the more interesting things the investigators found was in Allen West's cell — a road atlas of North America with the pages for Mexico removed. His cell also contained three hacksaw blades, three more spoons, and a chisel.

The scope of the escape was incredible and complicated. All those stolen or improvised tools. A virtual hardware store hidden behind blankets. Holes dug through 8 inches of concrete — with spoon handles and other rigged utensils. It was clear that the escapees had planned it for a long time. They had thought of everything. And they had a nine-hour head start.

The search expanded rapidly and was conducted by sea, land, and air. It covered the entire western United States. Highway patrol officers stopped and searched vehicles. Photos of the men appeared on newspapers all over the world. Where could they be?

The FBI believed that the men could have made it ashore and were on the run. But the men had no money, no clothes, and no food. They were career criminals. Surely they would make a mistake sooner or later — like getting caught in a robbery, for instance. The FBI carefully monitored the Anglin family home in Florida in case the men turned up there or made a phone call to their relatives.

A week after the escape, Warden Olin Blackwell received a postcard dated two days earlier. It said, "Ha ha we made it," and was signed "Frank, John, Clarence."

Blackwell gave the postcard to the FBI, but they didn't have enough handwriting samples from the prisoners to make a good comparison. They thought it was probably fake. But as the days went on and no bodies turned up, it seemed more possible that the men had successfully escaped.

That is certainly what Clarence Carnes and most of the other inmates believed. Carnes had escaped other prisons, so he knew it could be done. And he knew that his friends had worked hard on their plan. Alcatraz was not escape-proof, as the warden always claimed. Even though Carnes was still stuck inside, Alcatraz had been beaten. He didn't necessarily think that he would escape, but it felt good to know someone had. Even Alcatraz couldn't kill all hope.

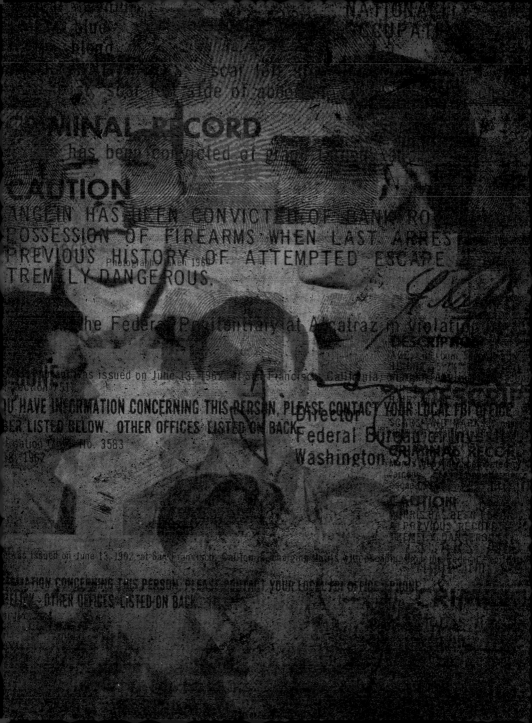

CHAPTER 2

LIFE ON THE ROCK

Frank Morris came to Alcatraz in January 1960 at 33 years old. He walked along the dock in handcuffs and leg irons accompanied by guards. The boat waiting for him, the *Warden Madigan,* bobbed in the choppy water. Morris, other prisoners, and the guards boarded the vessel, and the skipper pulled away from the dock. Alcatraz Island lay on the horizon, more than a mile ahead of them. It would be a long way to swim in frigid water.

Despite Morris's incarceration, he did not intend to stay long on Alcatraz. Morris was a robber. But what got him sent to Alcatraz were his many prison breaks. Before this, Morris had escaped from 11 prisons. Some men took up hobbies to pass the time in prison. Frank Morris hatched escape plans.

Thinking about escape was about the only way he knew to keep himself going. He needed something to hope for.

The *Warden Madigan* docked at the island, and Morris got off the boat and boarded a waiting bus, his leg irons clinking as he walked. The bus hauled up a twisty, narrow road toward the beige prison at the top of the hill. Once there, Morris climbed up a set of stairs. At the top a guard opened a gate to let him into a waiting room. Here, his chains were removed, and he was ordered to take off all his clothes. He stood naked as a doctor searched his body to make sure he wasn't smuggling anything in his ears, nose, mouth, or rectum.

Morris was then taken through several doors and down a hallway between rows of cells. At every step of the way, he scanned the area for hints or ideas about a possible escape. Could a person slip through that vent? Could he file through those bars? Everywhere he looked, he saw guards — more guards than he had encountered in other prisons.

In a basement shower room, he was ordered to wash up. He was given fresh clothes — including denim pants and a gray shirt — and led to his cell. There he received another set of clothes, as well as sheets, towels, a toothbrush, and other toiletries. Then he was left alone.

Morris sat in the dark and listened to his new home. He heard someone playing a guitar in another cell. He heard people chatting quietly. And he heard a whining sound. After some time, he realized it was the wind whipping across the island. Morris also looked out and cased his surroundings. There was a skylight — was there any way to reach it? He watched the guards make their rounds, and he timed them. He noticed which guards were armed and which were not.

Morris quickly got used to the dull routine on Alcatraz. In the recreation yard, inmates played softball, handball, chess, and other games. Men stood together in tight groups. It was cold outside, so each inmate was issued a heavy coat and a raincoat.

Cells were subjected to frequent thorough searches called shakedowns. Officers came in and turned over the mattress, cleared off shelves, and carefully inspected every corner.

Sometimes, without warning, an officer would come down the row of cells with a rubber mallet and hit each bar. If any bar made a duller sound than the others, he knew it had been tampered with, mostly likely filed or somehow cut. Guards made regular rounds, glancing into cells as the men read or painted or slept. Every convict and every guard in the place knew every sound. If you dropped something, everyone heard it and knew what it was. And if the guards heard anything unusual, they rushed over to investigate.

It was clear that anything hidden would have to be tucked away very carefully. Any illegal work such as cutting bars or digging concrete or making a tool would have to be done silently — and between guard rounds.

Within a couple of weeks, Morris was given a job cleaning vegetables in the kitchen. He also got moved out of his temporary cell into a permanent one on Cellblock B. His neighbor in the next cell was Allen West. West had been in Alcatraz for three years when Morris showed up in 1960. The men already knew each other from their time in an Atlanta, Georgia, prison years before. Where Morris was quiet and thoughtful, West was a talker and a bragger. For that reason, Morris didn't care for him at first. Like Morris, West had escaped before and was considered a risk. That's why the men had been sent to Alcatraz. It was deemed impossible to escape from Alcatraz.

After several weeks of cleaning vegetables, Morris got a new job as a library messenger. He delivered books and magazines to inmates throughout the prison. His next assignment was to the brush shop. There, he made brooms.

This last job was a promotion and earned Morris some income, which he could spend on magazines, books, art supplies — even musical instruments. The job also earned him "good time," meaning that the more he worked without getting into trouble, the more time was taken off his sentence.

One of the worst things about life on the Rock was the boredom. The daily routine never changed. Sometimes men would get in trouble just so they would be sent to the Treatment Unit, or TU. In TU, convicts were kept in their cells all day except for a shower and time alone in the yard. But at least it was different from the daily grind.

The worst offenses earned prisoners a trip to "the hole," also known as a Special Treatment Unit. In the hole prisoners had no privileges and never saw the light of day. They counted how many days had passed by the number of meals they were served.

In October 1960, Morris saw another familiar face in the dining hall — John Anglin, another man he knew from the Atlanta prison. Just like Frank Morris and Allen West, he was considered an escape risk because he'd escaped other prisons before.

John, or J.W., as he was known, came from a large, poor family. He'd committed most of his crimes in the company of his brothers Clarence and Alfred. They were robbers. Most recently, J.W. had been locked up in Leavenworth prison in Kansas with Clarence. The two planned to escape in bread boxes that were being shipped out. But a guard noticed how hard it was for the men to lift a box and ordered it opened up. Inside he found Clarence. J.W. was then sent to Alcatraz for his part in the plot. Clarence was sent to the isolation block in Leavenworth. Two months later, he was also sent to Alcatraz and assigned a cell next to J.W. The authorities believed it would be good for the two men to be close together so they could talk about family matters. They didn't have any concerns that the brothers would be able to escape. The Rock was, after all, inescapable.

According to Clarence Carnes in a later interview, an escape plan began to brew in Morris's mind soon after the Anglins arrived. The first thing that got him thinking was a story he heard from his neighbor, Allen West. West had told Morris about another convict who did electrical work up above Cellblock B years ago. The electrician had removed a fan motor from a vent shaft, and it had never been replaced. Except for the barred grille across it, the shaft was open.

Morris tucked this information away. He didn't have a safe way to get out of his cell and into the shaft — at least not yet. Then he made another discovery. The concrete walls that made up the cells were corroded. They could be scraped through over time with nothing more than a nail clipper, spoon, or other common utensil. How much could he dig before it would be noticeable? How could he hide it?

Other questions popped up. How big of a hole would he need to get through? How long would it take? Who, if anyone, should he invite into the plan?

And suppose he got through the concrete — then what? How would he get through the air shaft? How would he get off the island? He saw for himself how far it was to the mainland. Swimming there would be foolish. By the time he made it — *if* he made it — he'd be exhausted, confused, and hypothermic. He'd have no civilian clothes. Heck, he'd have no dry clothes at all. He'd have no money, no food, and no transportation.

There was a lot to figure out. But the plan had begun to take hold. The seed of hope had been planted.

A typical cellblock view on Alcatraz

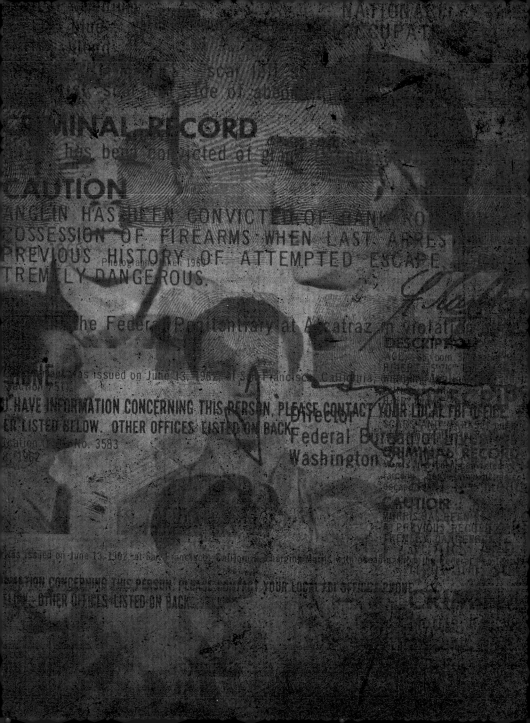

CHAPTER 3

DOWN THE WRONG PATH

Frank Morris mostly kept to himself. He didn't talk much, didn't share his thoughts with others — not unless it would help him. He could be charming when it served his purposes, or stay under the radar. Highly intelligent, he was a loner, and in many ways, he always had been.

Morris was an only child. His mother was 16 when she gave birth to him in 1926, and his father was a fugitive who had long since left her. Morris spent time in orphanages and foster homes until he finally ran away around age 11.

To get by on his own, Frank became a thief. He spent most of his youth in juvenile detention centers. There he learned how to be cunning and how to survive as a prisoner. When he was free, he went back to stealing to make his way.

As an adult, Morris added armed robbery to his list of crimes. Each time he was busted and sent to prison, he escaped. Each time he was recaptured, his sentence was all the longer because of the escapes.

Finally, in November 1955, wanting to get enough money to escape the country and start a new life, Morris broke into a bank in Louisiana with two partners. They used a torch to cut into the vault, which was booby-trapped with tear gas. In spite of the gassing, the three men escaped with about $6,000. After nine months they were caught, and Morris found himself in prison once more.

This time he was in the Atlanta Federal Penitentiary. Morris quickly got involved in a plan to escape, but the guards figured out something was up and searched Morris's cell. There they found a set of lock picks. After a stint in segregation, Morris got involved in another plan. This time, he and his accomplices were more careful. Using bar-spreaders they had made, one prisoner went to the cell house window during recreation time and spread the bars apart. When it was Morris's turn to slip through the opening, the entire window came loose and crashed to the floor, attracting the attention of the guards.

By that time, Morris had escaped so many times — or tried to escape — that authorities decided a big change was needed. So they sent him to Alcatraz.

The Anglin brothers were a lot louder and more outgoing than Morris. They came from a southern family with 13 or 14 children (sources differ) and grew up working as farm hands. They were poor, but the family worked hard. Their parents were described as honest. But poverty led the children to drop out of school and leave home looking for work to support the family.

The family moved to the small town of Ruskin, Florida, during World War II (1939–1945). By this time, J.W. and Clarence were in their early teens. They were only a year apart in age and had grown very close. They'd also become prone to adventure — and trouble. They began to steal, but when they were caught they were always quick to confess.

The brothers also loved to swim. When the family went to Michigan in May to work as cherry pickers, the boys would swim in Lake Michigan no matter how cold it was. Sometimes there was even ice in the water left over from the winter.

The young Anglin boys also built boats out of any scraps they could find. Perhaps their skills of swimming in frigid water and building boats came in handy years later.

As teens, the boys got into trouble for theft and breaking and entering. They wanted money for fancy clothes and dates, and they became quite skilled at busting into service stations after hours to steal cash and goods to sell. They avoided violence. But while they had a knack for crime, they had little skill for getting away with it.

Things got more serious when Clarence and another brother, Alfred, were arrested in 1951 for a burglary in Florida. They were adults now and sentenced to four years in a state prison. Six months later, the two brothers escaped from a road camp where they'd been working. It was the first of many escapes for both of them. They set into a pattern of committing a burglary, enjoying a short spree, getting arrested and sentenced, and breaking out.

In January 1958, J.W. got together with Clarence and Alfred, both of whom had broken out of prison and were in hiding. The three of them had wives or girlfriends, and all needed money. Naturally, they planned a bank robbery.

For the first time, they would stage a daring daytime robbery — using a real-looking toy gun. They targeted a bank in Colombia, Alabama. J.W. sat outside in the getaway car while Alfred and Clarence went in. Holding the pistol, Clarence convinced the bank president to fork over more than $20,000 in cash and travelers' checks. Then the men hid out in Ohio with their wives and girlfriends. They were caught five days later.

Because the money in the bank was insured by the U.S government, they had committed a federal crime on top of a state crime. The conviction was for armed robbery, even though the gun was fake. These factors meant stiff penalties for the brothers. Clarence and Alfred received a total sentence of 40 years, and J.W., the driver, received 35.

"They weren't bad guys," J.W.'s former girlfriend said. "They were just dirt poor."

Bad guys or not, the men were sent to federal prisons to do their time. All three went to the Atlanta Federal Penitentiary at first, but officials thought it best to separate Clarence from Alfred, since the two had escaped so many times together before. So Clarence was transferred to Leavenworth in Kansas.

Officials thought Alfred posed the greatest risk, so they moved J.W. out of Atlanta as well — and into Leavenworth. Reunited again, Clarence and J.W. immediately began plans to break out. Their attempt was the ill-conceived bread box plan that resulted in J.W.'s transfer to Alcatraz. A couple of months later, Clarence was busted for smuggling a letter for another inmate. It was not as serious as trying to escape, but it was enough to get him sent to Alcatraz with his brother.

Allen West was an escape artist too. He was serving his second term on Alcatraz. After the first, he'd been sent to serve the remainder of his sentence in a Florida prison. But West had escaped by holding a gun to the associate warden's head. When he was recaptured, he was sent back to Alcatraz.

West was originally from New York City but had spent much of his life in Georgia. He even spoke with a slight southern accent. West's favorite crime was stealing cars, and it was stealing a car and driving it across state lines that had got him sent to Alcatraz in the first place. Unlike the Anglin brothers, who avoided violence, West was known as a tough guy who was quick to attack. Across his fists, he had letters tattooed, one for each finger: H-A-R-D L-U-C-K.

In many ways, West was the key to the escape. He'd been in Alcatraz the longest — since 1957 — and he worked maintenance jobs. The jobs allowed him access to many areas of the prison so he could paint bars or walls, sweep up dust, or make minor repairs. While doing these jobs, West had cased much of the facility, and he was a talker. It was West who had told Morris about the missing fan motor in the ventilator shaft, putting the whole plan in motion.

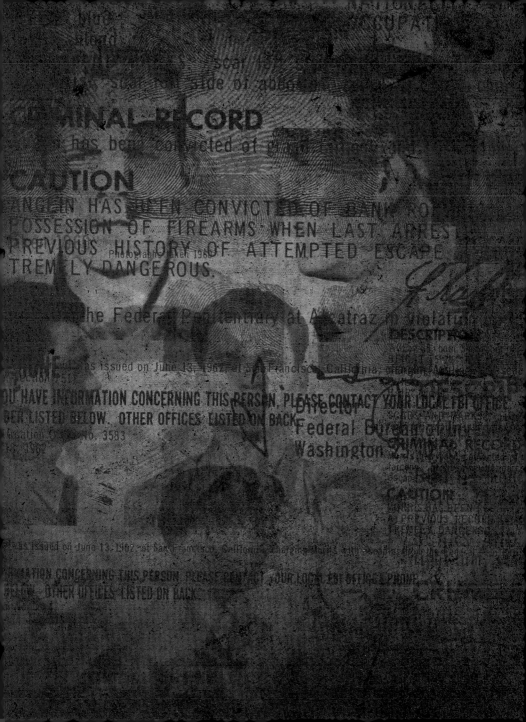

CHAPTER 4

TYING UP DETAILS

After West told Morris about the open shaft, and after Morris told West that he could chip away at the concrete around his cell vent, things began to move quickly. The Anglin brothers were brought into the plan. Like West and Morris, they had cells next to each other on Cellblock B. One from each pair could dig at his vent while the other acted as a lookout. Behind Cellblock B was the utility corridor they wanted to reach.

Many questions remained. The cells across the aisle from them in Cellblock A were empty, so no other prisoners could look directly in at them. But what about the prisoners in the opposite side of the utility corridor? Surely they would hear all the noise.

Allen West approached a prisoner named Bumpy Johnson. Bumpy was the leader of the African-American inmates, all of whom were housed in the cells behind them. He had been a powerful gangster before being locked up, and he was just as powerful inside Alcatraz. Bumpy assured West that nobody on his cellblock would say a word.

West was also able to produce two star drills that were hidden in the prison. Years ago, a shipment of woodworking tools had arrived at the shop in Alcatraz. Among them were the two star drills — drill bits with cutting edges in a star pattern that were especially made for cutting into concrete. They didn't require a machine; rather, they were meant to be hammered in by hand. The star drills were accidentally included in the shipment. An inmate quickly pocketed them and hid them away. West knew where they were and retrieved them. The star drills made the work of digging much easier. Some investigators believe there were other stolen tools used for digging as well.

According to Clarence Carnes, Allen West approached him next. Like West, Carnes was a veteran of the Rock.

He'd been there since 1945, when he was only 18 years old. Carnes had been convicted of kidnapping, murder, and — of course — escaping from a county jail. He knew even more of Alcatraz's secrets than West did. Even better, he worked in the library. That meant he had access to hiding places for banned items as well as the freedom to move around the cell house delivering magazines and books.

Carnes claimed West asked him if he wanted to join their plan. After carefully thinking it over, Carnes agreed, but he warned West that there was a lot of "heat" on him.

Carnes meant that the guards and officers tended to watch him carefully. That was because he'd taken part in an Alcatraz escape attempt some years earlier — one that had ended violently. Known as the "Battle of Alcatraz," six prisoners had strong-armed some guards and taken their guns and keys. But they didn't get the key to the recreation yard, which was how they'd planned to get out. It was clear at that point that the plan was not going to work, and three of the prisoners — including Carnes — went back to their cells to wait for officers to end the threat. But the others decided to fight to the death, preferring that to a lifetime in prison. They shot two officers to death and injured at least 14 others. Eventually the U.S. Marines and the U.S. Coast Guard were called in, and the riot was ended. The three prisoners who were still fighting were killed. Two of those who went back to their cells were sentenced to death. Carnes, who was only 19 at the time, had an extra 99 years added on to his sentence.

West talked it over with Morris and the Anglins. Eventually, they agreed it was too risky to invite Carnes into their plan. West had already risked a lot just by being seen talking to Carnes so many times over a few days. He broke the news to Carnes: He was out.

But according to Carnes, even being invited, even talking about the escape, was something to savor. He was heartbroken to be cut out, but he understood. He agreed to help his friends by providing information they needed. He worked with his connections in the library to hide and transport tools and other things for them.

Like information and hiding places, something else was

hard to come by on the Rock: privacy. But in 1961, the mess hall had been changed in a way that might have seemed unimportant at the time. The long tables that had set 10 men to a table were replaced with smaller, square tables. The new tables sat only four men. With the new setup, Morris, West, J.W., and Clarence Anglin could talk among themselves without being overheard. At each meal, they could quietly discuss their plan. They could update each other on how the digging was coming along. They could bring up challenges and brainstorm solutions.

It was at one of these meal discussions that Morris told the men to subscribe to lots of magazines. He told them to cut out pages that had ads on both sides — and cut them close to the binding so nobody would notice a page was missing. The men would use glue to layer the sheets to make cardboard. They would also need paint to make the cardboard look like the grille vents. The plan was to remove the real grille vents and stash them in the utility corridor behind the cells. Then they would replace them with the cardboard fakes.

They also discussed their digging progress at meals. The star drills made holes, but it would take ages to drill enough holes to pull out the grille. The answer was right there in the mess hall. The men stole spoons, bent off the bowls, and filed the ends sharp. With several holes drilled into one side of the vent, the men then hammered three spoon-wedges into the concrete using the heel of a shoe. The wedges loosened a long line of concrete that they pried out. That made progress much quicker.

Many of the men in Alcatraz owned musical instruments. They were allowed to play them in their cells between dinner and lights out. West, Morris, and the Anglins took advantage of this time to dig while the instruments provided camouflage for the noise. West had an accordion, which had another advantage besides the noise. It came in a big case that he stored in front of his grille. Anyone passing by would see only a small part of the grille; he carefully covered the area where he was digging. Morris liked this idea, and he ordered an accordion through the purchasing officer at the prison.

At night, the men dug. Morris laid down his heavy coat as a drop cloth to catch the dust and chunks that fell from his digging. That way no evidence would be left on the floor, and any bigger pieces that fell wouldn't make a noise as they hit the concrete floor. Sometimes he dug for so long his legs cramped, and he had to change position or stand up to stretch.

When he was finished for the night, he carefully gathered up the dust and rubble from his coat and put it in his pockets to discreetly drop in the recreation yard the next day. He was cautious only to dig so much that he could transport the waste without making a noticeable bulge in his pockets. He brushed any remaining dust off the coat into his sink and washed it down.

While West or Morris scraped away, the other kept lookout. The lookout made an agreed-upon sound when the guard — or "hack" — started heading their way, and the one digging would stop, slide the accordion case into place, and jump into bed. The Anglin brothers had a different setup. They ran a thin string from the cell of the lookout to the light switch in the cell of the digger. When the guard came, the lookout yanked the string and turned off his brother's light. That was the digger's signal to dash into bed.

One night, while West was digging, he made a clumsy mistake. He had his tools out on his bed when the hack was walking past. The only thing he could do was lean over the bundle to conceal them and hope the guard didn't wonder what he was doing. Luckily, the hack didn't pay any attention and kept on going. But then, as West got up, he dropped his star drill on the ground. Everyone heard it clang. He froze and waited for the hack to turn around. In the cell next door, Morris held his breath. But nothing happened. The hack paused for a few seconds, listened, then walked on.

Why hadn't he come back to investigate the sound? It made no sense. Clearly someone had something he should not have, but the hack ignored it. West thought maybe the guard was up to no good himself — perhaps *he* was sneaking something in that he shouldn't have. Sometimes guards could be bribed to carry messages or other things for prisoners. If that was the case with this particular hack, he would not want to make a discovery that would require other guards coming in. Or maybe he thought it was West's razor dropping to the ground. Razors did make a similar sound. Whatever the reason, the scare passed.

Not so coincidentally, the men all decided to take up painting as a hobby. They ordered paints, brushes, and canvases, and they painted portraits in their cells. The hacks sometimes stopped by to look at the paintings. Before long it seemed normal to see the men painting, and nobody thought it was unusual for them to order paints — even skin-colored paints. After all, the men were painting portraits.

But painting portraits was just a cover story. The real reason the men began to paint was so they could paint things that would help in their escape. First they painted the fake cardboard grilles in Alcatraz's signature mint green color to match the real ones. They also began to put together the dummy heads that they would soon need. They made plaster out of paper from magazines, concrete dust, soap, and any other materials they may have found laying around. Then they painted the heads to look like themselves.

Clarence Anglin had a job in the barbershop. He had no experience cutting hair, but like most jobs on the Rock, you didn't need experience. So what if you gave someone a less-than-perfect haircut? The advantage for Clarence was that he was able to pocket real human hair at the end of his shift. At night in his cell, he tied the hair into tiny bundles and glued the bundles onto the dummy heads. Just like the other details of the men's plan, each tiny bundle of hair required careful attention to detail.

View of the dug-out vent in one
of the escapee's cells

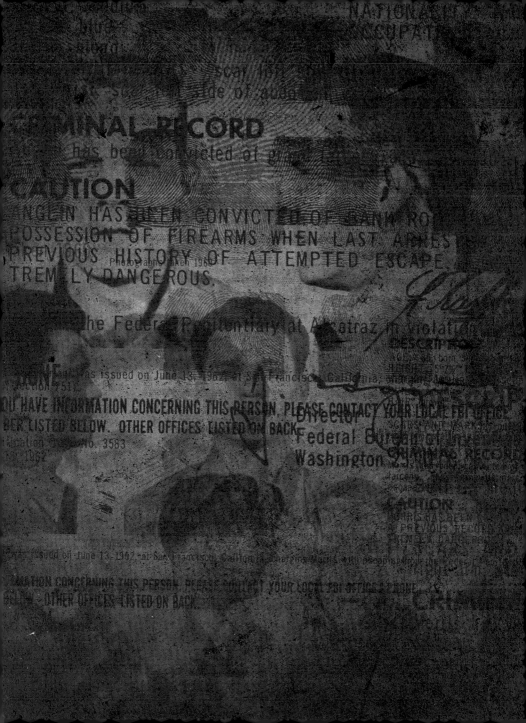

CRIMINAL RECORD

...has been convicted of...

CAUTION

...NGLEN HAS BEEN CONVICTED OF BANK ROB...
...POSSESSION OF FIREARMS WHEN LAST ARRES...
...PREVIOUS HISTORY OF ATTEMPTED ESCAPE...
...TREMELY DANGEROUS.

...he Federal Penitentiary at Alcatraz in violati...

...was issued on June 13, 1962, at San Francisco, California...

...OU HAVE INFORMATION CONCERNING THIS PERSON, PLEASE CONTACT YOUR LOCAL FBI OFFICE...
...BER LISTED BELOW. OTHER OFFICES LISTED ON BACK.

Director
Federal Bureau of Inv...
Washington 2...

...No. 3583

...was issued on June 13, 1962, at San Francisco, California...

...MATION CONCERNING THIS PERSON, PLEASE CONTACT YOUR LOCAL FBI OFFICE...
...OTHER OFFICES LISTED ON BACK.

CHAPTER 5

LOGISTICS OF THE BAY

Since Alcatraz became a federal penitentiary in 1934, there had been 13 previous escape attempts. Some, such as the Battle of Alcatraz, had been violent. Others were sneaky. None were successful. Most of the men involved were recaptured. Six were shot dead. Two men escaped the prison in 1937 but drowned trying to swim from the island to the mainland.

These previous failed attempts left most prisoners hopeless that they could ever flee the Rock. But not the Anglins, West, and Morris. The Anglin brothers were ready to break through the vents and make a run for it. But the more patient and intelligent Morris realized that previous escapees had put a lot of thought into getting out of the prison, but they had underestimated the difficulty of getting off the island. They needed a solid plan to get across the 1.25 miles of ocean between the island and the mainland.

The men faced two problems. First, they would need a way to cross the frigid, churning water without drowning or freezing. Second, they would need to get out of the area in a hurry without being noticed. If you're soaking wet and wearing a prison uniform, you tend to attract attention. Attention was something they did not want.

To solve the first problem, they decided to build rafts. The Anglin brothers had some experience with boats from their youth in Florida, and J.W. had learned from a magazine article how to work with rubber to shape and seal it. Clarence Carnes later took credit for finding a *Sports Illustrated* article that showed how to build a safe inflatable boat. He got it to West as soon as he found it.

The article also described several hand-operated pumps for inflating rafts. One of them looked very much like a concertina, an instrument similar to an accordion. Frank Morris ordered a concertina, and it arrived a few days later.

Since he already had the accordion, the hacks didn't think it unusual that he took a sudden interest in the new instrument. It just seemed as if his love of music was growing. He was able to remove the musical keys and rig the instrument to act as a bellows — or raft inflator.

J.W. was able to swipe raincoats from the supply room on rainy days during his job. He started his shift without a coat and grabbed one during his shift. The guard on duty at the end of his shift was different from the guard who was on duty at the beginning of it. He didn't know that J.W. had not been wearing a raincoat when he started. He began to swipe a raincoat every day, and sometimes two a day, wearing one beneath the other. At night, he pulled out the grille in his cell, which was now completely free, and left the coats for Morris.

By this time, Morris had opened his "door" all the way and had been in the utility corridor. In the dark of night, he had climbed up a series of plumbing pipes to the top and checked out the ventilator shaft, which he reported back had bars they would have to break through.

He also noticed that the convicts on the other side of the utility corridor were watching the men. They lay on the floor and peered through their own vents as the men dug at their "doors" and, later, climbed through. The men remembered Bumpy Johnson's promise that the inmates in his cellblock would not "rat" them out. But it made them very nervous to have so many convicts aware of what was going on. Somebody was bound to talk, or even accidentally reveal information. There was nothing to be done about it, though. They simply had to trust Bumpy.

As for the second issue, that of getting out of the area as quickly as possible, nobody knows for sure how or if they solved it. Considering the great care they took with every other step of the escape, they must have planned *something*.

In later interviews, Clarence Carnes claimed he believed that Bumpy Johnson played a role here. Johnson still had plenty of contacts outside of Alcatraz, and it was said that he could get things done — big things. Carnes said he noticed Allen West talking to him several times leading up to the escape.

On one side of the recreation yard was a set of wide rising steps. They were sort of like concrete bleachers that rose up from the floor of the yard to a big beige wall at the top. Inmates could sit on these "bleachers" and watch the handball and softball games, or just watch everything that went on in the yard. But there were unspoken rules. Only convicts with the highest ranking — cons who were feared and respected more than the others — could sit on the highest steps. From there they could see the Golden Gate Bridge and the skyline of San Francisco across the bay.

One man often found on the top step was Bumpy Johnson. There, he played chess with other inmates, often Clarence Carnes. It wasn't wise to approach Bumpy on the top step without permission. Anyone who went up that high unapproved would pay a price within days — he would find himself stabbed or at least badly beaten. According to Carnes, Allen West sought permission and was granted it.

Was Bumpy Johnson so well-connected that he could arrange for a boat to pick up the men? Many authorities on the escape don't think so. Besides, would he stick his neck out for four white men? Black and white men did not always get along well in the 1960s. For the most part they kept to their own groups. On top of that, Allen West was known as a racist and an agitator. He was often involved in fights between whites and blacks. On the other hand, there was a code of loyalty among prisoners on the Rock. According to Clarence Carnes, if Bumpy *could* do something to help the men, he *would*.

Frank Morris was also busy during his time in the recreation yard. Each day when he went outside, he made his way toward the area where the black convicts gathered. (In the cellblocks, the warden had the convicts separated by race. In the yard, they didn't have to be separate, but the black and white men tended to stick to their own groups.)

Morris wasn't there to socialize. In fact, he stood alone, staring off into the distance. It looked like he was simply daydreaming. But if you followed his gaze, you would see that he was looking out over the wall to the top of the cell house. He was casing the roof. There was the rain hood over the ventilation shaft they planned to climb through. At the side of the building, was a vent pipe from the kitchen that ran down to the ground. They could shimmy down that pipe to get off the roof. None of the guard towers offered a good view of the area. Morris gauged how much twine they would need to lower their raft and other supplies.

Meanwhile, Allen West was sewing in his cell at night. He removed the sleeves from raincoats and formed them into life preservers, which he sewed together with string, sealing the seams with rubber cement and tape. He had removed his grille vent so he could stash his sewing supplies and the life preservers in the utility corridor. But he did not widen up his "door" yet. He worried that once he removed that much concrete he would not be able to disguise the hole. With the grille out, he could reach into the corridor freely, but he could not fit his body through. It would be a simple job to kick out the weakened concrete until it was wide enough to fit through, which he would do on the night of the escape. And with so many of the details now being taken care of, that night began to feel very real — and very near.

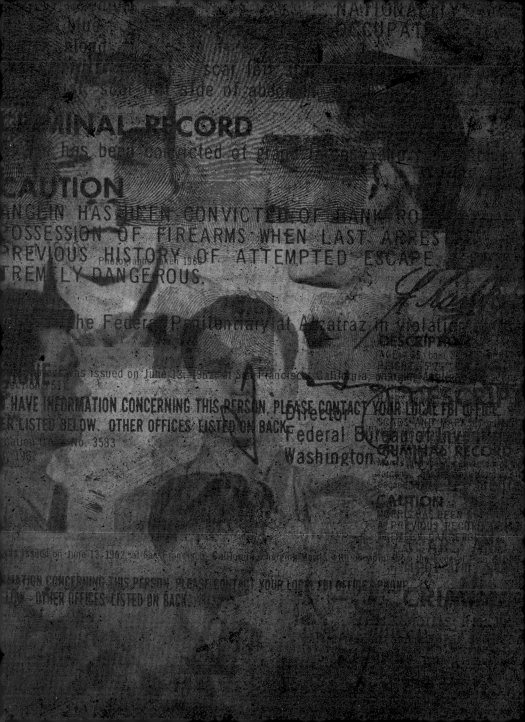

CHAPTER 6

HIDING IN PLAIN SIGHT

Soon both the Anglins were free of their cells too. They and Morris laid their dummy heads in bed with blankets wadded up to look like bodies. Then they crawled through the "door" in the back of their cells and scouted the corridor and ventilator shaft. They climbed the pipes, which formed a sort of ladder, as well as some wooden scaffolding that had been installed for plumbers and electricians to work on.

Besides the more than three dozen raincoats they had obtained by this time, they also had a sizable stash of other helpful items — twine, picks made from spoon handles, a flashlight, files, and more — that they stored on top of the cellblock and in the corridor.

But there was a problem. In order to work on their rafts, which were going to be 6 feet wide by 14 feet long, they would need more space. There was an open area on top of the cellblock that would be perfect for working. However, only ceiling-high metal bars ran along the side. A guard in the gun gallery could easily see anyone who went up there. In order to remove the roof vent to access the vent shaft — and certainly to work on their rafts — they would have to be able to use that area.

West came up with a plan. West worked in maintenance and often did jobs such as painting and cleaning different areas of the prison. He told cell house officer, John "Jerry" Herring, that he had been painting the area above the cellblock and noticed it was very dirty. Herring agreed and sent West to clean it up. Once there, West deliberately swept a lot of dust over the edge. Dust and paint flakes sifted down the front of the cells to the floor below, causing a great mess.

Before long, Lieutenant Maurice Ordway discovered the mess on the bottom floor and ordered Officer Herring to have it cleaned up. But there was one problem. West wasn't finished cleaning up top. What could be done to prevent more debris from falling?

West suggested hanging old blankets from the bars above to prevent the dust from going over the edge. Herring liked the idea and ordered blankets from the laundry. When Herring finished his shift that day, he was off for two days. Knowing this, West took advantage of the situation by talking with J.W., who worked in the laundry. West told J.W. to stall sending the blankets until the next day, and to send all the blankets he could.

The next morning, when Herring was off, two big hampers of blankets arrived in the cell house. West told the officer in charge that Herring had ordered them. The officer confirmed it, and right away West took the blankets to the top of the cellblock and began to hang them. There were 80 blankets altogether — enough to completely block the view of the top of the cellblock.

Morris and the Anglin brothers were impressed with West's shrewdness — and a little unsure. Would the guards really let those blankets stay there? It was an obvious security risk. They decided not to go to work up top until they knew it would last. So they waited for Officer Herring to return. When he did, he looked with surprise at the row of blankets and asked West if he really needed all of them. West cleverly responded that it was the amount he was given, and he assumed Herring had requested that many.

Shortly after that Lieutenant Ordway saw the blankets and immediately ordered them to be removed. Herring told West to take them down. But West had one last idea up his sleeve. West used his unique "people skills" and questioned why Lieutenant Ordway would have the right to make an order that went against what Lieutenant Herring had already okayed.

Herring thought about it and went back to Lieutenant Ordway to discuss the problem. West, Morris, and the Anglins did not know what they said. Whatever words were exchanged, the result was exactly what West had hoped for. The blankets stayed.

That night, just as they did every night, the men stood at the front of their cells for the 9:30 p.m. head count. Once everyone was counted, Frank Morris and Clarence Anglin pulled out their fake grilles and got their dummy heads from the utility corridor. Once they set the dummies in place in their beds, they squeezed through the "doors" and moved the fake grilles back in place. Anyone walking past their darkened cells would see that nothing was out of place.

The two men quickly scaled the pipes to the top level behind the tent of blankets. They inspected the roof vent and figured out that they would need to remove the steel bars welded into the frame within the shaft. More than an hour passed while they were up there, meaning a guard had gone past their cells on his hourly round. The dummies worked perfectly.

Over the next couple of nights they removed the ventilator grille and fashioned simple clamps to hold it in place while they were away. They were so careful, they made fake screw heads out of soap and set them where the real screws had been.

They realized that one big raft would be too clumsy to carry on the night of the escape, so they changed the plan to two smaller boats — one for Clarence and J.W. Anglin and one for Frank Morris and Allen West. Furthermore, the pontoons could be built here on the landing above the cellblock, but the boats couldn't be fully assembled until they pushed everything up through the vent shaft. They would have to do the final assembly on the roof. Each night, when the men finished their work, they hid the raincoats and other materials up in the vent shaft and replaced the grille. There was no sign whatsoever they had been up there.

Another problem to be solved was the fact that there were bars inside the roof vent before they reached the rain hood on top. The bars ran parallel across the circular frame. They were made from hardened steel that would not bend. West stole an electric hair clipper from the barbershop. Morris then converted the clipper into a drill. He and Clarence rigged an electric circuit from one of their cells to power it. But the drill wasn't strong enough to cut through the steel.

Next, West stole a vacuum cleaner motor by arranging for a distraction in the kitchen area. One inmate hit another over the head. While the guards attended to the fight, West smuggled out the vacuum motor and got it to his cell. Clarence Anglin and Morris converted the motor into a drill, but this one was too noisy. It sounded like a vacuum cleaner when they turned it on.

Finally, Morris hit on an idea that worked. Inspecting the wheel of bars one night with his homemade flashlight, he noticed that the outside ring of the wheel was embedded in the concrete with regular bolts. These bolts were made of soft metal rather than reinforced steel and would not be hard to cut with a file. Once they cut the bolts, they could push the entire ring up out of the shaft. After that, it would be simple to pop the rain hood off the top of the shaft and climb out.

By now, time was getting tight. The blankets would surely be coming down soon. They wanted to make their move before that happened. And the rumors spreading about their escape were becoming more and more abundant. Somebody was sure to let the secret out, either by accident or on purpose. The men had been planning, digging, building rafts, and assembling materials for months now.

According to Clarence Carnes, it was a miracle they had not yet been discovered.

On Monday, June 11, 1962, West came by the library and said hello to Carnes. Then he passed by again. Carnes later claimed he knew something was unusual.

"What's up?" he asked West the next time he passed.

"Nothing much," West said.

But Carnes could see that he was excited about something. Finally, West could keep the secret no longer.

"Oh, yeah," he said. "I forgot one little item . . . tonight we see the moon."

Carnes was thrilled. He wasn't going to see the moon, but the thought of his friends breaking through the vent and getting away gave him a surge of hope. If the men escaped, Carnes would have played a role in helping to "break the Rock." He felt dizzy with excitement.

The two men wished each other luck, and West walked out of the library. It was the last time they would ever speak to each other.

That night, Carnes lay in his bed and listened to the familiar sounds of the cellblock. He knew it would be hard for him to sleep. There was too much to think about.

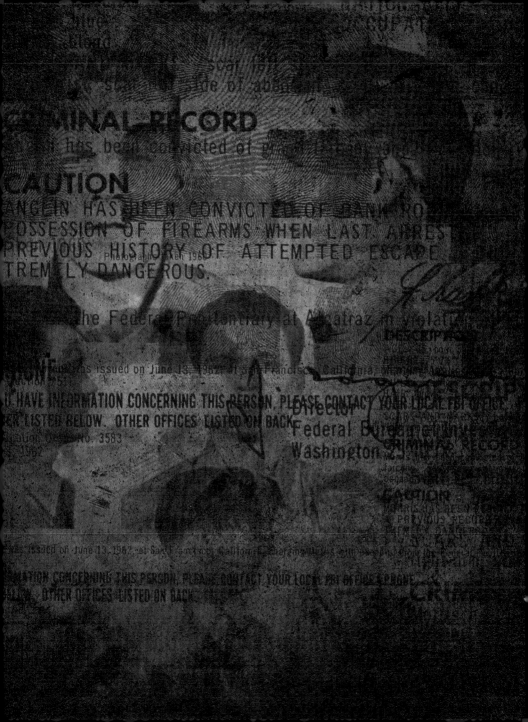

CRIMINAL RECORD

...has been convicted of ...

CAUTION

...ANGLIN HAS BEEN CONVICTED OF BANK ROB...
POSSESSION OF FIREARMS WHEN LAST ARRES...
PREVIOUS HISTORY OF ATTEMPTED ESCAPE...
TREMELY DANGEROUS.

Photograph taken 1960

...the Federal Penitentiary at Alcatraz in violati...

...was issued on June 13, 1962, at San Francisco, California...

...U HAVE INFORMATION CONCERNING THIS PERSON, PLEASE CONTACT YOUR LOCAL FBI OFFICE
...ER LISTED BELOW. OTHER OFFICES LISTED ON BACK.

...No. 3583

...1962

Director
Federal Bureau of Investigation
Washington 25

...was issued on June 13, 1962, at San Francisco, California...

...MATION CONCERNING THIS PERSON, PLEASE CONTACT YOUR LOCAL FBI OFFICE & PHONE
...LOW. OTHER OFFICES LISTED ON BACK.

DESCRIP...

CRIMINAL RECORD

CAUTION

PREVIOUS RECOR...

CHAPTER 7

THE ESCAPE!

At 7:30 p.m., the prisoners moved to the front of their cells to be counted. The guard walked past the cells, and when he finished his round, everyone was accounted for.

West lay in his bed in the same way his dummy would look, and waited. When the guard walked past, he moved slightly to show that he was real. Once the guard was safely past, West heard a soft, scraping sound behind his wall. He knew what that meant: Frank Morris was crawling out of his cell "door." West waited nervously. He wasn't to escape from his cell until the roof vent was open. West knew that once he opened his "door," he would not be able to patch it up well enough to fool the guards. It was a door for one-time use. If for some reason they ran into a problem and had to put off their escape, he did not want to be stuck with an obviously dug-out vent cover in his cell.

As for Morris, he deftly climbed the pipes, just as he had done every night over the past few weeks. J.W. and Clarence joined him. Clarence carried a waterproof sack he had fashioned, in which he stashed some important items: family photos and the names of people on the outside he could contact for help.

The three men crept behind their tent of blankets above the cellblock and boosted Morris into the vent shaft. Morris climbed up, filed through the bolts on the wheel of steel bars, and forced it up out of the top of the shaft. It clanged onto the roof, making a heavy metallic bang that everyone inside the cell house heard — including the guard on duty, Officer A.V. Young. Young called another officer in the control center to inquire about the sound. While he was on the phone, two more metallic clangs followed, very much like the first.

In the control center, Lieutenant Robert Weir turned on the paging system, which allowed him to listen via microphones to the entire cell house. He thought the sounds came from the hospital area and sent an officer to check it out. The officer found nothing out of place.

In his cell, Allen West waited tensely to see if the guards would figure anything out about the noises. When it became clear that they had decided it was nothing, he relaxed a little. Then he heard his name. It was Morris behind his vent grille.

It must have been music to West's ears. He may have smiled briefly before he got down and pushed with his feet against the grille. He expected it to come free fairly easily, but only one side popped out. He kicked again at the stuck side, but it held firm. He kicked again and again. It didn't move.

West's heart beat hard. He felt the one thing that had kept him going all this time — the hope for freedom — flicker. He knelt to the vent for a closer look. There was a steel bar reinforcing the grille on the stuck side. What was it doing there? None of the others had come across a reinforcing bar.

In a hard whisper, Morris asked what was taking so long. West explained about the bar and asked Morris to pull from his side. Working together, the men strained as hard as they could against the stubborn bar. But it was no use. It wasn't moving. West sized up the hole he'd made from kicking out the other side. It was too small. He would never fit.

After a few seconds of thought, Morris told West he would go get J.W. and Clarence and see what they could do.

And then he disappeared from the corridor. West knew that Morris would not return. The four men had made an agreement that they would not let one man put the whole mission in danger. If you couldn't do your part, you would be left behind. That was the deal that West had made. He had no one to blame but himself.

Instead of sulking about his blocked vent, West got to work. He figured he could bend the bar back and forth several times to snap it. He worked until his hands were torn and bloody. To West's surprise, Clarence Anglin did come to help him. He worked with West on the bar for a while, but they couldn't get it loose. He left West's dummy head in the corridor in case he got out. He could put it in place in his bed and catch up to the others. Then Clarence left him, just as Morris had.

The trouble West had with his vent meant they had to alter their plan. They decided to leave West's life preserver and part of a boat. They had built four pontoons, two for each boat. They took apart one of the boats and left one pontoon for West in case he got out. They would fix the remaining boat so that it had three pontoons and could support all three of them. Next they grabbed the paddles they'd fashioned out of plywood and some thin lumber they had scrounged. They left an extra one for West.

They shoved all their gear up the vent shaft above them and climbed up behind it. They scurried up the vent, pushing their gear ahead of them, and then they pushed everything out onto the roof and climbed out. They left the extra pontoon, life preserver, and paddle for West inside the air vent.

The men had been outside in the recreation yard, so simply breathing fresh air was not a new experience in itself. But breathing that air and feeling like free men — that was different. They filled their lungs with giant gulps of ocean air and ran across the roof toward the edge where

Morris had scoped out the kitchen stove vent pipe. Lights illuminated the wall, but they knew the closest guard shack was only occupied when the kitchen was receiving supplies. The Road Tower also had a clear view of the cell house wall and vent pipe, but it was not manned at night. Besides, there was no other way to go. They most likely tied their boat and other gear up in twine and lowered it down to the ground, and then climbed down the pipe after it.

The Dock Tower loomed 500 feet away, and it periodically flashed a light. The men crawled slowly along the prison wall, keeping their faces turned away so their pale skin wouldn't be reflected in the light flashes.

The men ran to a 10-foot fence and climbed over it. They clipped the barbed wire at the top with homemade wire clippers. There was no time to enjoy the feeling of the soft earth beneath their feet. Pulling the gear behind them, they scrambled down through the brush to the beach. No alarm had sounded, and nobody had seen them on the roof or on the ground. Now they were out of sight of the Gun Tower — they were free of the prison! They knew their dummy heads would keep their escape secret until morning. At this point, they only had to worry about getting across the bay. A dense fog floated over the water as they waded out and climbed into the raft.

People have argued for decades about what happened next. Did they take their raft all the way to San Francisco? Did they paddle to Angel Island, as other inmates claimed was their plan? Did they signal a boat and get picked up?

Allen West continued to work on that bar in the concrete. Finally, at around 1:00 a.m., he broke it. As quickly as he could, he squeezed through the hole, found the dummy head, and set it in his bed. Then he was back through the hole, up the pipes, and on top of the cellblock. He lifted himself into the vent shaft, where he found the pontoon the others had left for him. He climbed up to the top, pushed the pontoon out, and climbed onto the roof.

And there, lying on the roof, was his life preserver. But the other men had left him. He didn't trust that he could get off the island on his own. All of his work and planning had amounted to him standing alone on the roof of Alcatraz.

West climbed back into the vent shaft, down to the top of the cellblock, down the ladder of pipes, and into his cell. He put the dummy head back into the corridor and climbed into bed. He was exhausted and defeated. Prisoners in nearby cells later reported that they heard him crying and complaining that the others had left him.

The escapees left the vent grille on
the roof for investigators to find.

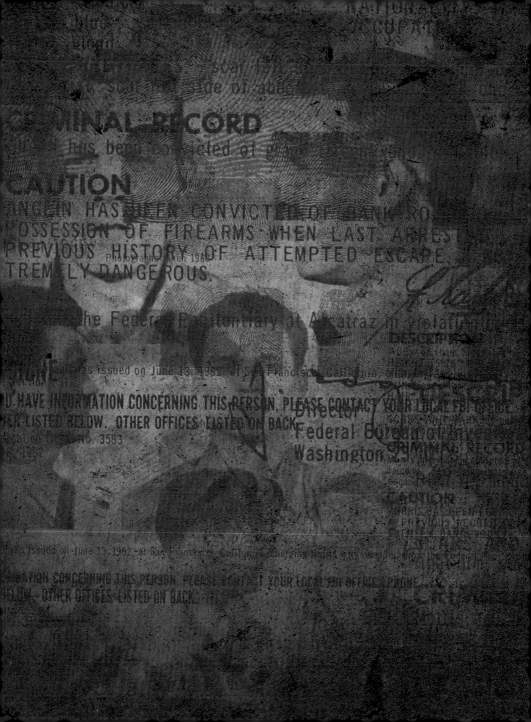

CRIMINAL RECORD

... has been convicted of ...

CAUTION

...NGLIN HAS BEEN CONVICTED OF BANK RO...
...OSSESSION OF FIREARMS WHEN LAST ARRES...
PREVIOUS HISTORY OF ATTEMPTED ESCAPE...
...TREMELY DANGEROUS.

...the Federal Penitentiary at Alcatraz in violatio...

...was issued on June 13, 1962 at San Francisco, California, charging...

...U HAVE INFORMATION CONCERNING THIS PERSON, PLEASE CONTACT YOUR LOCAL FBI OFFICE
...ER LISTED BELOW. OTHER OFFICES LISTED ON BACK.

...ION ...R No. 3583

Director,
Federal Bureau of In...
Washington 2...

...issued on June 13, 1962 at San Francisco, California...

...MATION CONCERNING THIS PERSON, PLEASE CONTACT YOUR LOCAL FBI OFFICE PHONE...
...ELOW - OTHER OFFICES LISTED ON BACK.

CHAPTER 8

FOLLOWING THE CLUES

When the 7:00 a.m. wake-up bell rang, Clarence Carnes and Allen West were already wide awake. Both were nervous and exhausted, especially West, who'd had what was probably the most frustrating night of his life.

Cellblock B stood for the 7:15 a.m. head count as usual. When it was discovered that Morris and the two Anglin brothers were missing, the alarm went out quickly. Guards combed the island — including every possible hiding spot inside the buildings and every cave and stand of brush outside. Bloodhounds sniffed the beach and led investigators to a spot on the north shore. There, the scent went cold.

Soon Alcatraz staff realized that the blankets hanging above Cellblock B had been key to the escape. It had been an outrageous mistake to provide such an obvious hiding spot for the escapees. When investigators went up there, they found the workshop that Morris, the Anglins, and West had established. A careful search of the roof turned up West's paddle as well as other tools and materials.

Once it was established that the three men were almost certainly off the island, the search expanded rapidly. The national press ran stories about the escapees, which included photos of the three men, and tips poured in from all over the country. One headline read, "OUT OF ALCATRAZ — BY A SPOON." People said they saw the men in all sorts of places, from Florida to Mexico.

Of course the news had also spread to the Anglin family in Ruskin, Florida. Clarence and J.W.'s mother, Rachel Anglin, had written a letter to Clarence on June 11 — the same day her sons escaped from prison. The letter contained news about a family wedding and an update on the local fishing. When she learned of the escape, she realized that Clarence had never received her letter, and she cried. She knew that she would probably never talk to her sons again.

Federal investigators descended on the Anglin family home. They secretly recorded the telephones in case J.W. or Clarence called. They read the family's mail. They followed family members, including Rachel, wherever they went, hoping to find clues. They came to the door and demanded answers to questions. The family did not cooperate, and the FBI did not ease up on them.

Two young boys, Ken and David Widner, were nephews of Clarence and J.W. They later said they could not go anywhere without the FBI following them. The federal agents harassed and intimidated them. Ken and David never forgot the constant pressure from the investigators, and they learned not to trust them. They would always hold a grudge against them.

As the two Widner boys got older, they continued to follow the case. They became obsessed with finding out what happened to their uncles.

Allen West knew there was no way he could hide his role in the escape. He would be interrogated relentlessly, and he would likely spend a long, long time in segregation.

While he waited on the roof that night, and later in his cell, he considered his options. He would have to talk. But if he said too much, he could endanger his friends' chances of success. He would have to say just enough to satisfy the investigators, but not so much that it would lead them to finding his friends.

When the escape was discovered, West stood up right away and showed the guards the "door" in the back of his cell. In fact, he claimed 100 percent credit for the escape plan. He said that it was he alone who had stolen all the raincoats, tools, and spoons. He had made the dummy heads. He had made the life jackets.

And then West told the investigators a story. He said that the men planned to reach the mainland, steal a car and guns, break into a clothing store to get something to wear, and drive away and separate. None of West's story panned out. It was probably a lie meant to throw the search off track.

All the cells on Cellblock B were searched. It turned out that two other prisoners had been chipping away at their vents too. June Heywood Stevens and Woodrow Wilson

Gainey had cells on the third level and had learned of the escape plan. They had wanted to join the men.

When questioned, Gainey admitted that he and Stevens had been trying to escape with the others. But West found out and told them to stop digging. They were on the third floor, for one thing, and they would be crawling out of their vent holes into a three-story drop-off, with only pipes to grab onto. It was too difficult, and the risk of falling and getting discovered was too great. West also worried about them being discovered if chips of concrete fell the three floors down or the plumbers saw the work they were doing from the utility corridor. The men stopped when West asked them to and never resumed.

Gainey also told investigators that the escapees intended to steal a helicopter. Frank Morris had read a book about how to fly one. He said they planned to separate, then get together in the future and rob banks. None of this was true.

For days, helicopters hovered over the bay and up and down the coast. Patrol boats prowled through the water, poring over beaches, cliffs, rocks, and piers. The FBI sent eight cruisers to join the search. Divers searched underwater all around Alcatraz. But the three men did not turn up — dead or alive.

Three days after the escape, a homemade paddle was discovered near Angel Island. It was made from plywood and painted green — the same green as almost everything in Alcatraz. The paddle matched the one left behind for Allen West. The location of the discovery indicated that the men had headed for Angel Island. But had they made it? If so, how did they get off of the island? Where did they go next?

The day after that, a U.S. Army debris boat was moving between Alcatraz and Angel Island. These boats pick up trash and other junk floating in the water. As it passed between the two islands, it picked up Clarence Anglin's waterproof bag containing photos and contact information. The bag was made of the same raincoat material as the life preserver and the pontoon left behind for West. Officially, the FBI determined that this bag was very important to the three men. There was no way they would have intentionally let it go. They must have drowned.

Eventually, all three of the life preservers were found. One was found near Alcatraz, one was found close to Angel Island, and one was found way out beyond the Golden Gate Bridge, nearly out to sea. It seemed likely that the jackets had deflated and the men had slipped under the icy water to drown. But their raft was never recovered, nor were their bodies.

According to statistical records, two out of every three people who go missing in the San Francisco Bay will eventually be found. The fact that none of the bodies were recovered does have statistical significance. But it doesn't rule out the idea that all three men drowned near the same place, their bodies drifting out to sea on the same current.

Some investigators — and certainly many inmates and relatives of the Anglins — believed that the men probably intentionally dropped the bag, hoping that authorities would come to the conclusion that they had drowned.

As the weeks and months went by, tips kept coming in, most of them providing no real leads. One was the postcard addressed to the warden and supposedly signed by the escapees. Another was a phone call made to a lawyer in San Francisco. The caller claimed to be John Anglin, and he said he would surrender if the lawyer would get him his "day in court." The lawyer, Leslie MacGowan, had done work for an Alcatraz inmate once years ago and gotten him freed. The man's name spread among other Alcatraz inmates after that, and he represented several over the years. J.W. may have gotten his name from someone inside. But investigators could not learn anything from the phone call, and the person never called again.

A worker on a freight ship heading out past the Golden Gate reported seeing a body in the water around the time the men escaped. He said it was floating face down and looked to be wearing what might be prison denims. But nobody else had seen the body, and he had not reported it until weeks later. One family reported that they saw a raft with three men in it out near San Pablo Bay, the northern end of the San Francisco Bay. They said that a speedboat had come by and possibly picked up the men from the raft and sped away. But when the FBI checked it out, they found nothing.

One tip pointed to the possibility that the men escaped successfully. It was illegal for any boat to be within 200 yards of Alcatraz Island. But police records show that there was a boat within a mile or two of the area on the night of the escape. A police officer reported seeing the boat sitting silently with its lights off around 1:00 a.m. After some time, the motor came on, the lights came on, and the boat drove under the Golden Gate Bridge, out to sea.

Deeper investigation revealed that the men had been studying Spanish during the months they were planning their escape. Some federal investigators believe their plan all along was to head to Mexico or South America, where they could blend into the daily life without being noticed.

Tips continued to come in. But the men were never found, and soon the investigation dwindled.

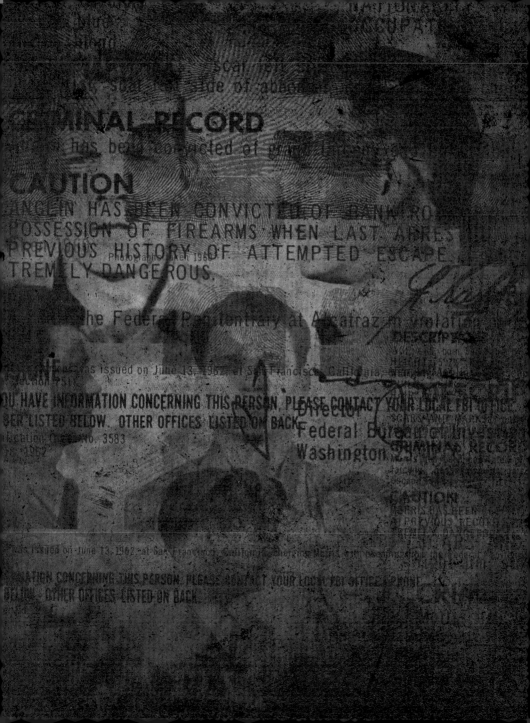

CRIMINAL RECORD

CAUTION

ANGLIN HAS BEEN CONVICTED OF BANK ROB
POSSESSION OF FIREARMS WHEN LAST ARRES
PREVIOUS HISTORY OF ATTEMPTED ESCAPE
TREMELY DANGEROUS.

the Federal Penitentiary at Alcatraz in violation

is issued on June 13, 1962 at San Francisco, California,

YOU HAVE INFORMATION CONCERNING THIS PERSON, PLEASE CONTACT YOUR LOCAL FBI OFFICE
BER LISTED BELOW. OTHER OFFICES LISTED ON BACK

ication Order No. 3583

Director
Federal Bureau of Investi
Washington 25

Issued on June 13, 1962 at San Francisco, California

MATION CONCERNING THIS PERSON PLEASE CONTACT YOUR LOCAL FBI OFFICE
BELOW. OTHER OFFICES LISTED ON BACK

CHAPTER 9

THE YEARS TICK BY

In December 1962, six months after the escape, Rachel Anglin received a Christmas card in the mail. It was signed with her sons' names — John and Clarence. It must have filled her heart with joy to see those names and believe that they had escaped. The following Christmas another card arrived signed by John and Clarence. In 1964, for the third year in a row, a Christmas card arrived from the brothers. Not only that, but Rachel received flowers from an anonymous sender every Mother's Day until she died.

Rachel and her family, including her grandsons Ken and David Widner, believed that John and Clarence were behind the Christmas cards and flowers. They believed that J.W. and Clarence had lived.

Rachel died in 1973, and the FBI attended her funeral in case J.W. or Clarence made an appearance. Nobody who looked like the two fugitives attended, but two unidentified women did show up. They were very tall and looked strong. They wore long dresses and heavy makeup, and they didn't speak to anyone. Immediately after the service, they disappeared before anyone could talk to them, including the FBI agents. Many have suggested that this was Clarence and J.W. Anglin come to pay respects to their mother.

The FBI kept the investigation open for 15 years. They followed leads all over the world and kept tabs on the Anglin family. But they never found the three men, and in 1979 they declared them officially dead and closed the case.

The U.S. Marshals reopened the case in 1993 when an inmate named Thomas Kent gave an interview to a TV show called *America's Most Wanted*. He said that Clarence Anglin's girlfriend had agreed to meet them on shore and drive them to Mexico. Officials weren't convinced this was true. Even so, a spokesman for the U.S. Marshals said, "We think there is a possibility they are alive."

In 1989 a promising tip was sent to the U.S. Marshals by an anonymous woman identified only as "Cathy." She had seen an episode about the Alcatraz escape on the TV show *Unsolved Mysteries*. On that episode, artist renderings were presented of what the men would likely look like at the time — almost 30 years since they'd last been seen. Cathy called a tip line and said she had visited with a man living near the town of Marianna, Florida, who looked exactly like Clarence Anglin. She said Frank Morris was with him.

Authorities didn't know whether to believe her at first, but she provided details about the escape and correctly identified Anglin's height, eye color, and other physical features not generally known by the public. Also intriguing was the fact that the Anglin brothers had grown up in a Georgia town just a few miles from Marianna and had family nearby. It seemed like a logical place for them to go.

Cathy also said that she knew how the escape had succeeded. She said that members of the Ku Klux Klan had arranged to have a car waiting for the men in San Francisco. According to her story, the men had driven far away from the area by the time authorities figured out they were missing in the morning. Then they split up, with Morris and Clarence Anglin settling in Marianna.

Cathy gave a location for the fugitives' home, and U.S. Marshal "Mac" McLendon immediately set out to check the story. He spent weeks searching around the rural area surrounding Marianna, but he couldn't find any information about Anglin or Morris. The tip, though it had seemed promising, was a bust.

As for the Anglin family, most of them believed that J.W. and Clarence made it out alive. In 1992 an old family friend, Fred Brizzi, told the family that he had run into them in Brazil in 1975. And he had a photo to prove it. The photo shows two men standing next a huge anthill. The men look remarkably like J.W. and Clarence. For Ken and David, only boys when their uncles escaped, this confirmed what they had hoped all along: The men had survived the escape.

Brizzi was a drug smuggler who was doing business in Brazil at the time. He claimed he ran into John Anglin at a bar and was taken back to his and Clarence's farm.

He said they had a lake on their land and showed him how to body surf holding onto a rope behind a boat. Brizzi said that was how they escaped across the bay — by lassoing a boat transporting guards off the island. FBI records show that 120 feet of electrical cord had been stolen from the prison. Had they used it to rope the guard boat?

If Brizzi had this information that would be so important to the family, why did he wait so long to tell them? He said he believed that if he gave the information or photo to the family sooner, the federal investigators would have found out. He was keeping the Anglin brothers safe by sitting on his secret. In 1992 he felt it was finally okay to share it. Brizzi died a year later.

Fred Brizzi's wife of 20 years, Judith Brizzi, cast doubt on his story. She had seen the photo in question, but Fred never mentioned who was in it. She had divorced Fred and reminded investigators that he was a criminal and, therefore, not trustworthy.

Ken and David Widner, who had grown up in the shadow of the mystery, offered to share the photo with investigators many years later, in 2015, in exchange for a favor. The favor had to do with another Anglin brother, their uncle Alfred.

Alfred Anglin had stayed in prison for his whole sentence without trying to escape, and by 1964 he was finally up for parole. When family members visited him in prison, he was excited about getting out. He also revealed that he had heard from Clarence and J.W. and planned to visit them when he got out. A few days later, Alfred tried to escape and was electrocuted on a security fence. He died.

The Anglin family smelled something fishy. Why would Alfred try to escape after all this time, when his parole was right around the corner? It didn't make sense. They didn't believe he had tried to escape. Rather, prison officials had heard him talking about Clarence and J.W. and they tried to get him to tell them what he knew. When he wouldn't talk, they beat him to death. Then they threw his body on the electric fence and made it look like a failed escape attempt.

Ken and David Widner called up Art Roderick, the one U.S. Marshal investigator who had managed to gain their trust.

"We feel like we've found the right person we can trust in Art and felt comfortable enough to share it," Ken Widner said.

Roderick met Ken and David in Ruskin, Florida. The Widner men showed Roderick the Christmas cards the family had received, but these didn't interest Roderick much. They could very easily be fakes. Then they showed him Brizzi's photo. That got Roderick's attention.

Roderick had investigated this case for decades. He was eager to get it solved. So he asked the brothers if he could take the photo and have it analyzed. But Ken and David would not give up the photo — not without a favor. They wanted to have Alfred Anglin's body exhumed from its grave and examined. Did it have signs of physical trauma, as if he'd been beaten? Roderick wanted the photo, so he agreed to the deal. Alfred's body was pulled from the ground and examined. It did not show any signs of physical abuse.

While they had the body, they took the opportunity to solve another mystery. Back in 1962, around the night the men escaped, a body had been recovered from the bay.

Some had speculated that it might have been one of the escapees, but there was no proof. Investigators ran DNA testing on the body from the bay and on the body of Alfred Anglin to see if there was a match. But the drowning victim did not have any Anglin DNA. They also tested a member of Frank Morris's family. There was no match there, either. The dead man found in the sea was not Clarence or John Anglin or Frank Morris.

Meanwhile, Roderick had the photo from Fred Brizzi tested. A forensic artist found eight different points on each face that matched the brothers' mug shots. He declared that the photo was "highly likely" to be the Anglin brothers. Still, Roderick was not totally convinced.

"It's a lead," he said, "but I would like some more pieces of evidence."

He added, "I'm still holding to my original opinion that, until we have 100 percent confirmation they survived, that it's most likely the brothers drowned in San Francisco Bay. Forensic artists are not like DNA or fingerprints; it's not an exact science."

Nevertheless, the photograph gave Roderick hope. Though he has retired, that hope drives him to continue investigating on his own until he solves the case, just as hope drove the prisoners on the Rock. Ken, David, and the rest of the Anglins also feel driven by hope — the hope that J.W. and Clarence defied the odds and survived their escape.

"This is absolutely the best actionable lead we've had," Roderick said of the photo. "I truly believe we're going to close it."

Until then, the mystery lives on.

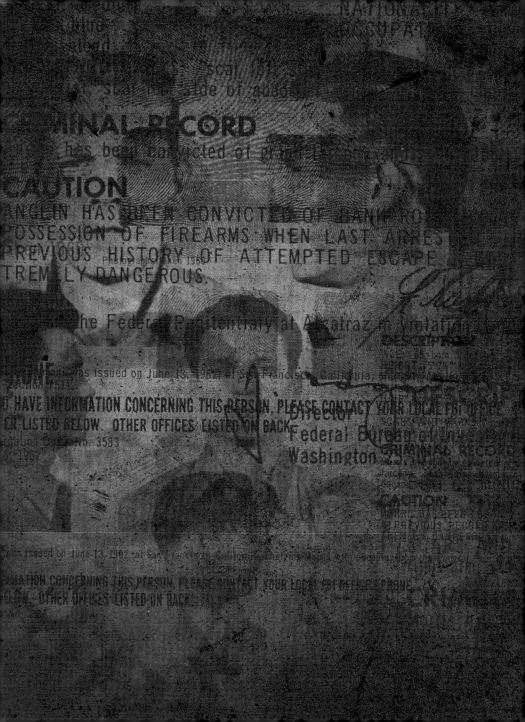

EPILOGUE

Months after the escape, then U.S. Attorney General Robert Kennedy announced that the prison at Alcatraz would be closed. In a way, this was a big part of the legacy of the escape. For men such as Clarence Carnes, breaking the Rock, even by someone else, was a way to get off of it. Life in Alcatraz was miserable, and the thought that one day he could get out of there was the only thing that kept Carnes and other inmates going — that hope.

So where did they end up?

Allen West cooperated in the investigation into the escape. He was interviewed once by Alcatraz officials and twice by federal investigators. In return, he was not charged for participating in the escape. He was transferred several times to other prisons and finally released in 1967, after which he was arrested for grand larceny. He was serving a life sentence in the Florida State Prison when he died of an abdominal disease on December 21, 1978, at 49 years old.

Clarence Carnes, who was serving a life sentence on top of a 203-year sentence, was nevertheless paroled in 1973 at age 46. But he violated his parole and went back to prison, where he died of complications related to AIDS in 1988.

Bumpy Johnson was released in 1963 and returned to Harlem, New York, where he was a powerful and popular gangster. He died of a heart attack in 1968 at age 62.

U.S. Marshal Art Roderick is retired but continues to investigate the escape from Alcatraz. He is hopeful that the case will be solved in his lifetime.

Ken and David Widner live in Florida, and they continue to wait. If their uncles survived, they would be in their mid-80s now.

Starting in October 1973, Alcatraz became a tourist attraction. Each year, more than 1.3 million people ride the ferry across the bay that Morris and the Anglins set out to cross so long ago. Visitors can tour the island and buildings, including the cell house. Former convicts and guards narrate the recorded tours. Rangers and other volunteers lead the guided tours.

Today visitors can tour Alcatraz and get an up close view of the cells.

BIBLIOGRAPHY

Alcatraz History

www.alcatrazhistory.com

Alcatraz: Search for the Truth. History Channel video.
https://www.youtube.com/watch?v=Uo7wDky-c84

Babyak, Jolene. *Breaking the Rock.* Berkeley, Calif.: Ariel Vamp
Press, 2001.

Boyle, Louise. "EXCLUSIVE: Alcatraz escapees 'had wives and
children in Brazil', their family claims - and they want their
sentences commuted so they can 'come home' after 53 years,"
Daily Mail, October 15, 2015.

http://www.dailymail.co.uk/news/article-3273273/Alcatraz-
escapees-Clarence-John-Raglin-wives-children-Brazil-family-
claims-want-sentences-commuted-come-home-43-years.
html#ixzz48wMjF0Nd

Bruce, J. Campbell. *Escape from Alcatraz.* Berkeley: Ten Speed
Press, 2005.

DeNevi, Don. *Riddle of the Rock.* Buffalo, New York: Prometheus
Books, 1991.

Escape! Breakout from Alcatraz. History Channel video.
https://www.youtube.com/watch?v=DO153ueJX1A

Graff, Amy. "New claim: Alcatraz escapees might have survived, could still be alive." *SF Gate,* October 13, 2015.

http://www.sfgate.com/news/article/New-evidence-Alcatraz-inmates-suspected-dead-6566124.php

McFadden, Robert D. "Tale of 3 Inmates Who Vanished From Alcatraz Maintains Intrigue 50 Years Later" *New York Times,* June 9, 2012.

http://www.nytimes.com/2012/06/10/us/anniversary-of-a-mystery-at-alcatraz.html?_r=0

Thompson, Paul. "EXCLUSIVE: 'In all the years we were together he never talked about those men' - Widow of drug smuggler who claimed he ran into the Alcatraz escapees in Brazil says husband was a 'con artist'." *Daily Mail,* October 16, 2015.

http://www.dailymail.co.uk/news/article-3276052/In-years-never-talked-men-Widow-drug-smuggler-claimed-ran-Alcatraz-escapees-Brazil-says-husband-artist.html#ixzz48wMQBvA6

An overhead view of
Alcatraz Island

Alcatraz Island, as viewed
from San Fransisco

Allen West's mug shot, circa 1957

U. S. PENITENTIARY
ALCATRAZ
1130
4 14 54

U. S. PENITENTIARY
ALCATRAZ
1476

U. S. PENITENTIARY
ALCATRAZ
1441

U. S. PENITENTIARY
ALCATRAZ
1485

Mug shots from left to right:
Clarence Anglin, J.W. Anglin,
and Frank Morris

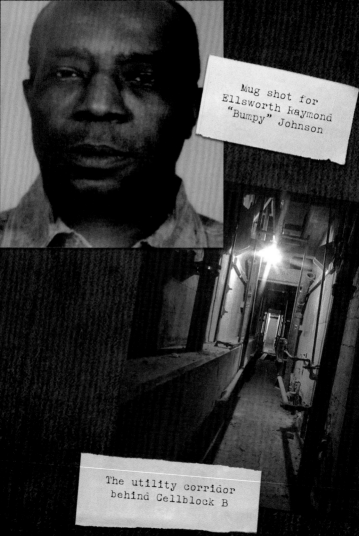

Mug shot for
Ellsworth Raymond
"Bumpy" Johnson

The utility corridor
behind Cellblock B

Four-to-a-table seating in the Alcatraz mess hall

Concrete "bleachers" in the Alcatraz recreation yard

A typical Alcatraz cellblock

One of the dummy heads posed
inside an escapee's cell

Clarence Anglin's
cell, showing a hint
of the dug-out vent

The "workshop" above
Cellblock B, hidden
behind the blankets

A selection of stolen
and handmade tools
hidden by the escapees

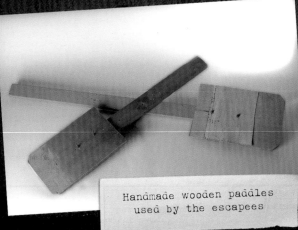

Handmade wooden paddles
used by the escapees

The homemade life
preserver left behind
for Allen West

An investigator
inspecting the
dismantled vent grille

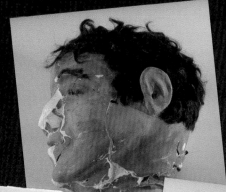

John Anglin's dummy head
was made out of soap
chips and bed sheets.

Frank Morris's dummy
head was the most
realistic-looking.

Clarence Anglin's dummy
head was nicknamed
"Oscar" after one of the
Anglins' uncles.

Allen West's dummy head
was nicknamed "Oink."

Age-progressed images of
Frank Morris, Clarence Anglin,
and John "J.W." Anglin beneath
their mug shots

GLOSSARY

accomplice (uh-KOM-pliss)—someone who helps another person commit a crime

atlas (AT-luhss)—a book of maps

case (KAYS)—to inspect a location, usually with the intention of committing a crime there at a later date

cellblock (SEL-blok)—a unit of a prison consisting of a number of cells, usually joined together to form one structure

chisel (CHIZ-uhl)—a tool with a flat, sharp end used to cut stone or wood

civilian (si-VIL-yuhn)—a member of society not serving in the military or held in the prison population

convict (KAHN-vikt)—someone who is in prison because he or she has been convicted of a crime

corridor (KOR-uh-dur)—a long hallway or passage in a building or train

corrode (kuh-RODE)—to destroy or eat away at something little by little

debris (duh-BREE)—the scattered pieces of something that has been broken or destroyed

federal (FED-ur-uhl)—relating to the U.S. government

fugitive (FYOO-juh-tiv)—someone who is running from the law

hypothermia (hi-puh-THUR-mee-uh)—a life-threatening condition that occurs when a person's body temperature falls several degrees below normal

incarceration (in-kahr-suh-REY-shuhn)—a period of time in prison

inmate (IN-mayt)—someone who has been sentenced to live in a prison or other institution where one is under supervision

offense (uh-FENSS)—a crime or rule infringement

penitentiary (PEN-uh-ten-shee-air-ee)—a prison for people found guilty of serious crimes

riot (RYE-uht)—a large gathering of people who use violence to show their anger

scaffolding (SKAF-uhld-ing)—temporary framework or set of platforms used to support workers and materials

segregation (seg-ruh-GAY-shuhn)—the practice of separating a person or group of people from others

smuggle (SMUHG-uhl)—to move something secretly and often illegally

ventilator shaft (VEN-tuh-lay-tuhr SHAFT)—passageways to move air throughout a building

warden (WORD-uhn)—someone in charge of a prison

CRITICAL THINKING USING THE COMMON CORE

1. What do you think were the biggest mistakes made by the guards at Alcatraz that allowed the three men to escape? (Key Ideas and Details)

2. Do you think that Frank Morris and the Anglin brothers succeeded in their escape? What evidence supports your opinion? (Integration of Knowledge)

3. This books starts by telling about the morning of the escape, then details the events that led up to it, and finally goes over the investigation. Did your opinion of what happened to the escapees change between the first chapter and the last? If so, what details changed your mind? (Craft and Structure)

ABOUT THE AUTHOR

Eric Braun writes fiction and nonfiction for kids, teens, and adults, but sometimes he still dreams of being a professional skateboarder. He lives in Minneapolis with his wife, sons, and dog.

READ MORE

Berne, Emma Carlson. *World's Scariest Prisons.* New York: Scholastic Inc., 2014.

Hyde, Natalie. *Alcatraz.* Crabtree Chrome. New York: Crabtree Publishing Company, 2013.

Oliver, Marilyn Tower. *The Infamous Alcatraz Prison in United States History.* In United States History. Berkeley Heights, N.J.: Enslow Publishers, Inc., 2015.

INTERNET SITES

FactHound offers a safe, fun way to find Internet sites related to this book. All of the sites on FactHound have been researched by our staff.

Here's all you do:

Visit *www.facthound.com*

Type in this code: 9781515745518

FactHound will fetch the best sites for you!

INDEX